Lost in the ANTARCTIC

by Kevin Blake

Consultant: Mike Sparrow, PhD
Scott Polar Research Institute
University of Cambridge, United Kingdom

New York, New York

Credits

Cover © Volodymyr Goinyk/Shutterstock and © Warren Goldswain/Shutterstock; 4, © AFP/Getty Images; 5, © National Geographic/Getty Images; 6, © Ashley Cooper/Alamy; 6BR, © Images & Stories/Alamy; 7, © National Geographic/Getty Images; 8CL, © Gordon Wiltsie/National Geographic/Getty Images; 9, © AFP/Getty Images; 10–11, © Colouria Media/Alamy; 12CR, © Thinkstock; 12B, © National Geographic Image Collection/Alamy; 12–13, © Steffan Christmann/Corbis; 14CR, © MEPL; 14B, © Hulton Archive/Getty Images; 15, © 2D Alan King/Alamy; 16CL, © Thinkstock; 16B, © Royal Geographic Society/Alamy; 17, © Thinkstock; 18, © Shackleton Epic/PA Images; 18–19, © Yongyut Kumsri/Shutterstock; 20CR, © National Library of Norway; 20B, © MEPL; 21, © Lett Milling/Getty Images; 22, © British Antarctic Survey; 23, © Andreas Strauss/Getty Images; 24, © National Geographic Image Collection/Getty Images; 25, © Doug Allan/The Image Bank/Getty Images; 26, © Peter Rejcek/National Science Foundation/U.S. Antarctic Program; 26–27, © Photodynamic/Shutterstock; 28, © Picture Dress/Alamy; 29, © Michael Ashley.

Publisher: Kenn Goin
Senior Editor: Joyce Tavolacci
Creative Director: Spencer Brinker
Photo Research: Brown Bear Books Ltd

Library of Congress Cataloging-in-Publication Data in process at time of publication (2015)
Library of Congress Control Number: 2014009085
ISBN-13: 978-1-62724-289-9 (library binding)

For more information, write to Bearport Publishing Company, Inc., 45 West 21st Street, Suite 3B, New York, New York 10010. Printed in the United States of America.

10 9 8 7 6 5 4 3 2 1

Contents

Blinded!

In March 1990, Japanese dog trainer Keizo Funatsu was part of a team that used dog sleds to explore one of the coldest places in the world—**Antarctica**. The team was only 16 miles (26 km) away from completing their 3,725-mile (5,995 km) journey when they stopped to set up camp for the night. It was late afternoon when Keizo left the camp to feed the sled dogs. Suddenly, the clear sky turned dark gray.

Keizo Funatsu (top row, left) and his team, along with their sled dogs

Swirling snow and wind began to pound Keizo's face. The **blizzard** made it impossible to see, and Keizo soon lost sight of camp. He cried out in the darkness, "I'm here! I'm here!"—but there was no response. The howling winds were so loud that no one could hear him. As the snow piled up around him, Keizo's heart began to sink. He was lost in Antarctica!

Sled dogs have thick coats of fur and strong muscles, making them perfect for traveling long distances in cold, icy Antarctica.

The **continent** of Antarctica is in the southernmost part of the world. It's one-and-a-half times bigger than the United States.

Buried Alive

Keizo had no time to waste. It was -25°F (-32°C) and his feet were starting to freeze. He dug a two-and-a-half foot (0.76 m) deep **ditch** in the snow and crawled inside for warmth. Within seconds, the blowing snow covered his body. Inside the snowy hole, Keizo could hear only the thumping of his heart.

A snow ditch like the one Keizo took shelter in

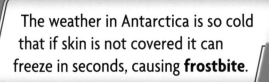

The weather in Antarctica is so cold that if skin is not covered it can freeze in seconds, causing **frostbite**.

Frostbitten fingers

As night fell, Keizo had one goal: to stay alive. That meant both keeping warm and trying to get help. He curled up into a ball to keep from freezing. Every twenty minutes or so, he jumped out of the ditch and waved his arms in the air, hoping that someone would see him. Then powerful **gusts** of wind would blow Keizo away from the ditch and force him to crawl back inside to warm up.

In Antarctica, blizzard winds can blow as fast as 199 miles per hour (320 kph).

Search Party

When Keizo didn't return to camp that night, his teammates began to worry. Team leader Will Steger organized a **search party**. The five men marched through the storm, each holding a section of a long rope so they would not get separated. After a long night of searching, their hopes began to fade.

Will Steger, the team's leader

As Will and the other members of the search party marched, they shouted Keizo's name and listened carefully for a response.

Not far away, Keizo worried that he might never be found. Early the next morning, however, he heard what sounded like a voice. He had a choice: run toward the noise or wait. It was now or never. He ran through the snow until five shadowy figures appeared. They were his teammates. The men grabbed Keizo and cried together. He was saved!

A grateful Keizo, at far right, with his teammates

A World of Ice

As Keizo learned, there are few places more dangerous to be lost in than the Antarctic—a large ice-covered area in the southern part of the world. Within this area is a large continent called Antarctica, where the **South Pole** is located. Antarctica is the coldest, windiest, and iciest place on Earth. At the South Pole, temperatures in the winter average -75°F (-59°C). The freezing temperatures can lead to **hypothermia**, frostbite, and even death.

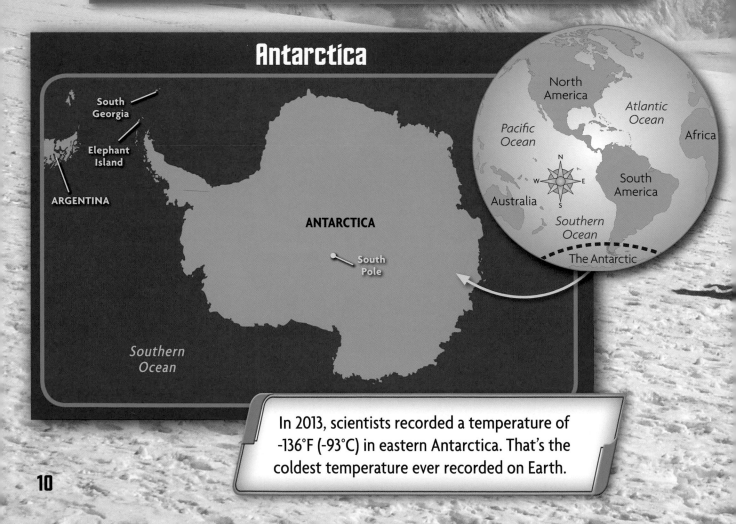

Antarctica

South Georgia

Elephant Island

ARGENTINA

ANTARCTICA

South Pole

Southern Ocean

North America

Atlantic Ocean

Pacific Ocean

Africa

South America

Australia

Southern Ocean

The Antarctic

In 2013, scientists recorded a temperature of -136°F (-93°C) in eastern Antarctica. That's the coldest temperature ever recorded on Earth.

Massive sheets of ice cover nearly 99 percent of Antarctica. These shifting sheets can be more than 15,000 feet (4,572 m) thick. Underneath the ice is a rugged landscape that includes steep mountains, low valleys, and even volcanoes.

Part of the ice sheets covering Antarctica

Land and Sea

Because of the continent's ice and freezing temperatures, few animals are able to survive on land in Antarctica. Most animals, such as seals and penguins, live in or near the sea, where it's slightly warmer. The sea is also home to fish and other small animals that penguins and seals feed on.

An Antarctic fur seal

Just off the coast of Antarctica is the Southern Ocean, where most of the area's wildlife lives, such as this leopard seal.

A leopard seal can weigh up to 840 pounds (381 kg) and stretch out to 11 feet (3 m) in length.

One animal that is able to survive all year long on land is the emperor penguin. How? The birds have a thick layer of fat that keeps them warm even in freezing temperatures. During storms, the penguins huddle together in large groups, protecting each other from the harsh wind and cold.

Emperor penguins huddling together in Antarctica

Trapped by Ice

Since Antarctica is such a cold and difficult place to survive in, why would anyone want to travel there? For British explorer Ernest Shackleton, it was the chance to do what no one had ever done before: cross Antarctica using teams of sled dogs. On August 1, 1915, Ernest and his 27-person crew left London, England, to set sail for Antarctica aboard a ship called the *Endurance*.

Ernest Shackleton

The *Endurance* after first setting sail for Antarctica

In December, as the *Endurance* approached Antarctica, the water became dangerous. Huge chunks of ice called **ice floes** appeared in the water. The captain tried to steer the ship around them, but it was too difficult. Ice slowly surrounded the wooden **vessel** and pressed on its sides. Ten million tons (9 billion kg) of ice pushed against the 144-foot-long (44 m) ship, until its sides snapped like toothpicks.

A member of Ernest's crew examines the destroyed ship.

When the *Endurance* was destroyed, help was more than 1,200 miles (1,931 km) away.

Escape to Elephant Island

Ernest gave the order for his men to save what supplies they could and **abandon** the ship. The crew was forced to set up camp on the nearby ice floes. For nearly six months, they struggled to survive, sleeping in cold, wet sleeping bags and hunting seals and penguins. They waited and waited, hoping the wind would move the ice so that it would open up a passageway for their lifeboats to sail through.

Ernest's crew waiting for the ice floes to move and give them a chance to escape

The ice floes that the men camped on cracked and broke apart as the seawater moved underneath them. Soon, the men were living on a small ice floe that was only 50 yards (46 m) across.

Ice floes

Finally, a passageway formed one dark night. All 28 men set out in three tiny lifeboats, hoping to find safety. Frostbite and gray saltwater **boils** marked the men's faces. After seven days, they reached an **uninhabited** island called Elephant Island. They were on land for the first time in 497 days.

Elephant Island

Rescue

Ernest and his men were not safe yet, however. Help was still more than 800 miles (1,288 km) away on the island of South Georgia. Leaving most of the crew behind, Ernest and five volunteers got into one of the lifeboats and set sail. Using only the sun and stars as their guides, they battled waves up to 36 feet (11 m) high to reach the island. Ernest would stop at nothing to save his men.

Ernest and five men battled rough seas in a tiny boat, similar to this one.

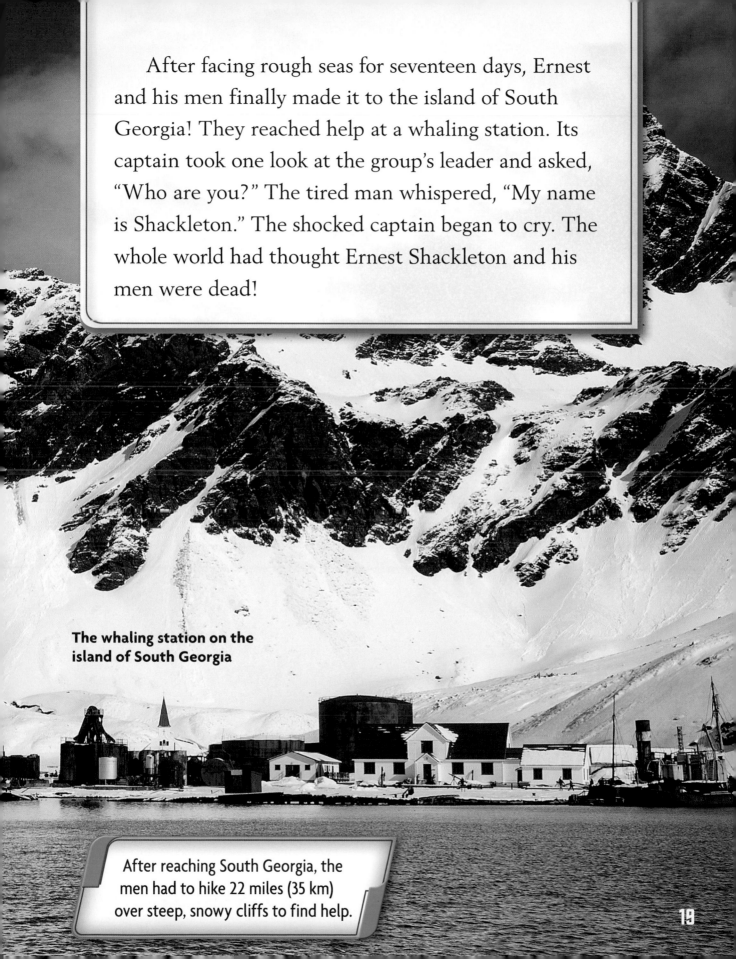

After facing rough seas for seventeen days, Ernest and his men finally made it to the island of South Georgia! They reached help at a whaling station. Its captain took one look at the group's leader and asked, "Who are you?" The tired man whispered, "My name is Shackleton." The shocked captain began to cry. The whole world had thought Ernest Shackleton and his men were dead!

The whaling station on the island of South Georgia

After reaching South Georgia, the men had to hike 22 miles (35 km) over steep, snowy cliffs to find help.

Journey into the Past

The Antarctic's **climate** is so **brutal** that even today's airplanes, radios, and snowmobiles can't protect explorers from its dangers. In December 1993, a group of four Norwegian adventurers went to Antarctica. Their goal was to travel by snowmobile to retrieve **artifacts** left by Roald Amundsen, a Norwegian explorer who in 1911 became the first person to reach the South Pole.

The snowmobilers hoped to recover a tent that explorer Roald Amundsen left at the South Pole in 1911.

Roald Amundsen

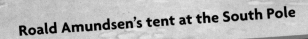

Roald Amundsen's tent at the South Pole

The Norwegian team sped across the Antarctic ice on snowmobiles toward the South Pole. Suddenly, one team member disappeared. Then another. They had fallen into deep dark cracks in the ice's surface called **crevasses**. Panicked, the other members set off a **distress beacon**. This alerted Steve Dunbar and the other members of a search-and-rescue team about the disaster. Would Steve and his team arrive in time to help the men?

Snowmobilers race across Antarctica.

A Dangerous Mission

Steve and his team of skilled rescuers boarded an airplane at McMurdo Station on the coast of Antarctica and flew to the accident site. As they got closer to the South Pole, Steve saw many dangerous crevasses below. Finally, in the distance, he spotted the Norwegians' camp.

A Twin Otter plane, much like the one that carried the search-and-rescue team, flies over a field of crevasses.

Even landing the plane was dangerous. Just 40 feet (12 m) away from where the plane touched ground were crevasses the plane could have fallen into.

Getting to the camp, however, was nearly impossible. Because of all the crevasses, the plane was forced to land two miles (3.2 km) away. The rescuers then had to slowly hike over the icy snow to reach the Norwegians. They fell into crevasses more than 20 times. Thankfully, they had roped themselves together so they could pull each other out of the deep cracks. Four hours later, they finally arrived at the site. Sadly, the scene they found was **grim**.

Members of a search-and-rescue team help each other get around a crevasse.

Into the Crevasse

The rescue team learned that one of the missing snowmobilers had been able to climb out of the crevasse he had been trapped in. He had broken ribs and had suffered a **concussion**, but he was recovering. The other snowmobiler, however, was still trapped inside another crevasse. Steve knew he had to do all he could to rescue him.

A man walks above a deep Antarctic crevasse.

The Norwegians showed Steve where the man was trapped. Steve used a rope to slowly lower himself into the dark crevasse. Soon, he was 120 feet (37 m) below the ice's surface. The space was so narrow that Steve had to hold his breath just to squeeze through. Using a light on his helmet, Steve looked down and saw a horrible sight. It was a frozen, lifeless arm reaching up toward him!

A person lowering himself into a crevasse in Antarctica

Steve had no choice but to leave the snowmobiler's frozen body in the ice. The body is still trapped in the ice today, more than twenty years later.

Getting Home

Even though Steve was upset by his tragic discovery, there were still three Norwegians who needed the rescuers' help. Steve quickly taught the men how to travel safely on the ice by roping themselves together. The two-mile (3.2 km) trip back to the plane took more than three hours. When they finally reached the plane, everyone breathed a sigh of relief. They were finally safe. Without the heroic work of the rescuers, there may have been no survivors at all.

A search-and-rescue team helps an injured Antarctic traveler.

Antarctica will always challenge daring explorers such as Keizo Funatsu, Ernest Shackleton, and the team of Norwegian adventurers. Luckily, for some of these explorers, there are brave rescuers, like Steve Dunbar, who will risk their lives to help them. As long as explorers come to the Antarctic, there will always be heroic stories of extreme survival!

Each year, more than 4,000 scientists from around the world visit Antarctica to study it.

Antarctic Survival Tips

If you plan to visit the Antarctic, follow these tips for survival.

☑ Get ready for cold weather. Even in the warmest months, the weather can suddenly fall to -50°F (-46°C). To protect yourself, cover every part of your body with warm clothing. The cold weather can freeze your skin in seconds.

☑ Use eye protection. The strong glare from the ice can damage your eyes if you don't wear special goggles or sunglasses.

☑ In the event disaster strikes, have a survival bag handy that includes extra water and a tent in case you are **stranded** for several days.

This man is dressed warmly and wears eye protection to face the harsh Antarctic weather.

- Keep moving if you feel like your body is starting to freeze. Exercises like jumping jacks or sit-ups will keep your blood flowing throughout your body.
- Travel with a friend so that you can watch each other for signs of hypothermia, such as patches of frozen white skin or talking in a confused way.
- Bring a shovel in case you need to build a snow ditch during a blizzard.
- Like Keizo, you may need to find your way back to camp in a blizzard. In order to be prepared, practice walking without being able to see. Put a plastic bucket over your head and see if you can find your way around. Make sure a friend is nearby so that you don't walk into anything!

This scientist practices searching for people during a blizzard by placing a bucket over his head.

Glossary

abandon (uh-BAN-duhn) to give up and leave

Antarctica (ant-ARK-tih-kuh) the southernmost area of land on Earth

artifacts (ART-uh-*fakts*) objects of historical interest that were made by people

blizzard (BLIZ-urd) a storm with very strong winds, temperatures below 20°F (-7°C), and hard-blowing snow that lasts for at least three hours

boils (BOILZ) inflamed swellings of the skin

brutal (BROO-tuhl) tough

climate (KLYE-mit) the usual weather of a place over a long period of time

concussion (kuhn-KUSH-uhn) a temporary brain injury caused by a heavy blow to the head

continent (KON-tuh-nuhnt) one of the world's seven large landmasses

crevasses (kruh-VASS-iz) deep open cracks in ice

distress beacon (diss-TRESS BEE-kuhn) an electric signal expressing that help is needed

ditch (DICH) a narrow hole dug into the ground

frostbite (FRAWST-bite) the freezing of skin due to exposure to extreme cold

grim (GRIM) depressing or worrying

gusts (GUHSTS) strong blasts of wind

hypothermia (hye-puh-THUR-mee-uh) a condition in which a person's body temperature becomes dangerously low

ice floes (EYESS FLOHZ) floating sheets of ice

massive (MASS-iv) giant; huge

search party (SURCH PAR-tee) a group of people formed to find someone who is lost

South Pole (SOUTH POHL) the most southern end of the Earth, located in Antarctica

stranded (STRAND-id) stuck somewhere without a way to leave

uninhabited (uhn-in-HAB-uh-tid) having no people living there

vessel (VESS-uhl) a ship or large boat

Bibliography

Lansing, Alfred. *Endurance: Shackleton's Incredible Voyage.* New York: McGraw-Hill (1959).

Wagner, Tom. "Tips for Surviving in Antarctica," *New York Times*. March 28, 2008. (www.nytimes.com/2008/03/28/nyregion/28teacherbox.html?ref=nyregion&_r=0)

Walker, Gabrielle. *Antarctica: An Intimate Portrait of the World's Most Mysterious Continent.* Boston: Houghton Mifflin (2013).

Read More

Friedman, Mel. *Antarctica.* New York: Scholastic (2009).

Hooper, Meredith. *Antarctic Adventure: Exploring the Frozen South.* New York: DK (2000).

Kimmel, Elizabeth Cody. *Ice Story: Shackleton's Lost Expedition.* New York: Clarion (1999).

Learn More Online

To learn more about surviving in the Antarctic, visit
www.bearportpublishing.com/Stranded!

Index

About the Author

Kevin Blake lives in Portland, Oregon—far away from Antarctica— with his wife, Melissa, and his one-year-old son, Sam. Like Antarctic explorers, Sam likes to practice walking around with a bucket on his head.